Pause and Reflect

Mary Anne Kessler

BookLeaf
Publishing

India | USA | UK

Presentation by *BookLeaf Publishing*

Web: www.bookleafpub.com

E-mail: info@bookleafpub.com

ISBN: 9789360947675

First edition 2024

Motherhood

Waiting on your arrival
Tired snuggles and baby coos
Words, teeth, and day of school
All the firsts

Cuddled up reading to you, then you reading to
me
Always growing, learning, becoming, changing
Carpool and practices
Watching you try your best-
sometimes winning sometimes not
Dynamics change

Wanting you to stay
Knowing you will pave your own road
Away from me
Waiting on your return

Buffett

So many options - which to choose
Groups of people intersecting
Comfort or adventure all await
Single, married, kids?
Service, Education, Faith, Career
Pictures capture the moment
Memories and bonds
Sticky Rice, Fish and Chips, Ceviche, Poutine,
Lobster, Gelato…
Never full
Next?

Iowa

Hundreds of miles of heat and hills
The smell of money and church lady pie
Smiles and laughs, sunburns and craft beer
Town squares ready to welcome and entertain
Looking forward to pork chops and Ice cream
sandwiches
Sore muscles, road rash, memories

New

I planted a garden for the bees
In a time of seclusion and anxiousness

native, natural, nectar, noticing, nestled

I weeded, trimmed, added more plants
A corner of possibility among uncertainty

Navigating, N95, no travel, new normal

I returned to routines of life
A reminder of quarantine, a garden for the bees

Bricks

5

Helmets and shields of past sets
Creatively repurposed
Frogs become the column
Paddles become the petals
Orchids, roses, wildflowers, succulents
Everlasting or dismantled to build again
Bringing my childhood into adulthood
Creating centerpieces

Self Maintenance

Not broken
Not new
Time to revamp
Massage, adjust, upgrade, and alterations
Replacing the old
Taking time to slow time
Fresh air
Breathe
Reconnect
Ready for another day

Midlife

So much depends on
Roots and highlights

They notice
They comment
30 or grandma?

Glimpse

One of the most awe inspiring sights
The sky as dusk falls
Dark azure dotted with stars
white, yellow, orange, red, pink
Evening rainbow gradients
painter and canvas
watching as night approaches

Time

9

My breathe catches mid-thought

To be able to reverse time

Another day with loved ones

Chances to undo mistakes

Being young and hopeful

would I still be me?

2-4-6-8-2

magic
talons and horns
hoofs rumble earth and air
terrifying or fantastic
arcane

Hobby

Recline
Escape the drudgery
Allow yourself to see new lands
Dangerous encounters
Immersed in life
Natural wonders, loves, betrayal
Grieving conclusion

In retrospect

Life's path unknown
Take the road less traveled
Take what's behind door #2
Passion Prudent
Adrift Anchored
Steady Sporadic
Brawn Brains
Never sure
Second guessing
Decisions made
Content with myself

Whole

There are so many dreams I had for myself
All based from others' lives
There are so many deadlines to meet and goals
I'd hope to reach
All the lists and tasks and milestones laid out
ahead
There are so many ideals shape decisions
All taking me in someone else's shoes
There are so many ways to live authentically
All of them worthy of admiration
There are so many dreams I have for you
All based on building your own life

Hold On

Some lessons in life make us stronger and teach
Trials are not to destroy us but to refine
Blessings renew our spirit and give us hope
Battles develop a mindset and values
May you always listen for your own voice
May you always find your own reflection
May you always feel loved

Unalome

The path of life
Filled with chaos
Twists and turns
Highs, Lows, everything in between
Waiting for peace and enlightenment
Your time racing to the buzzer
Ride the waves
Lean into the curves
Keep pressing on
Life is lived in the change

Stained Glass

Feeling more broken
Trying without success
Holding it together
Finding ways to connect
Shards and slivers come together
A beautiful mosaic of life

Pause

Yearning for hope
Over-thinking and second guessing
Under pressure
Mistakes and errors pile up
Almost giving up
Tomorrow feels far away
Take a moment to pause;
Embrace this challenge
Remember, "You Matter!"

Crazy Ladies You Call Mom

I hope you will remember the fun we had
Driving to play in waterfalls
Camping near the train tracks
Spook's Cove and Jellystone
Counting U-turns
Driving in the storm until we couldn't see and
park by a building

Climbing rocks and descending into caves
Natural spring swimming pool
Thunderstorms that lit the sky
Packing in the middle of the night to beat the
next storm- just barely
Driving until we couldn't stay awake any longer
and finding a hotel

Cable car up a mountain
Shops and streams
Elk in the yards and on the street
Pancake the size of a pizza
Climbing rocks again and again
Driving until we couldn't wait any longer to eat
and finding an Italian restaurant in some small
town

Pushing on to sleep under the stars
Ring of campers nestled together
Our oasis away from home
Climbing more rocks and stomping through
more streams
Wild animals roam
Driving around bends tight and steep making
memories with these crazy ladies you call mom

www.ingramcontent.com/pod-product-compliance
Lightning Source LLC
La Vergne TN
LVHW050313200726
843509LV00015B/3299